CHOOSING TO BE
CLOSE

CHOOSING TO BE CLOSE

Fill Your Life With Rewarding Relationships

GORDON McMINN WITH LARRY LIBBY

MULTNOMAH PRESS
PORTLAND, OREGON 97266

Cover design and illustration: Hilber Nelson

CHOOSING TO BE CLOSE
© 1984 by Multnomah Press
Portland, Oregon 97266

Library of Congress Cataloging in Publication Data

McMinn, Gordon.
    Choosing to be close.

    1. Friendship.   2. Interpersonal relations.   I. Libby,
Larry.   II. Title.
BF575.F66M37   1984   158'.2   84-3297
ISBN 0-88070-053-X (pbk.)

84 85 86 87 88 89 90 — 10 9 8 7 6 5 4 3 2 1

To Donna

Who chooses to be my wife and friend

Contents

Introduction 9

1. Because You're Worth It 11

2. Avoid Withdrawing
    Face the Option of Risk 27

3. Avoid Placating
    Wean Yourself from the Expectations of Others . . 39

4. Avoid Intruding
    Wait until the Door Is Opened 51

5. Learn Giving
    Find the Richer Way of Life 63

6. Learn Receiving
    Accept What Only Others Can Give 73

7. Learn Inviting
    Ask Others in to Get Acquainted 83

8. Learn Contributing
    Reduce the Distance through Shared Goals 93

9. Working for a Living . . . or for a Life? . . 101

Introduction

IT'S HARD TO SAY what prompted me to write a "how to" book on relationships. I can think of several possibilities. One, I work with people at a family counseling center. Many of the people who come to see me seem to be struggling with questions such as: "What are some principles I can use to build better relationships?" And "How can I avoid destroying a relationship that really means a lot to me?" I'd like to help these sincere, often hurting people discover ways to reach their goals.

Two, a growing number of men and women have feelings of alienation or isolation in this rapidly changing, increasingly technical world of ours. I'd like to contribute some ideas to encourage these apprehensive ones to risk building some meaningful friendships.

Three, I've had times of loneliness and discouragement myself. In my own quest for fulfillment, I have pondered questions in my mind for days as I seek to learn and to grow.

There must be other reasons, but these seem important for now. Particularly that third reason. It sounds funny, but somehow by helping you, I help myself.

My colleague and close friend, DeLoss Friesen, has made a significant contribution to this effort. Dee and I work together at the same counseling center. We've shared many hours of interaction over countless cups of coffee. And when you're engaged in that kind of idea-level interaction over at least five years ... who can take credit for what emerges?

As you begin this book, let me make two very important requests of you.

First, *look ahead instead of behind you.* It's much more beneficial to determine where you choose to go than to dwell on where you've been. There *is* hope. So please, look ahead.

Second, *focus on yourself, not on those around you.* I know ... it's difficult. I can't number the times I have had to remind myself of this. But I have to come face to face with the fact that it is not within my power, nor is it my responsibility, to change anyone else. I have the freedom and the right to choose for myself, to make my own decisions. And so do you. There are alternatives before you—some very helpful and productive ones. So as we share this brief journey, focus on yourself!

The resources you need to build better relationships are within you ... and within reach. God put them there. As you read, I pray that He will help you discover them.

Gordon McMinn

Chapter 1

Because You're Worth It

SETTING ASIDE THE vivacious cheer-leader role she wears among her peers, an attractive high school girl writes: "In today's world I see myself as a 'well brought-up kid.' But my feelings are somewhat different. I have no pride in what I am doing here. I am more or less a lost individual."

A young man in the same high school pens these words: "Because I am pessimistic, I tend to downgrade many things, one thing being myself. I see myself as a tremendously small person looking through a window on the outside world, the sophisticated life. I cannot envision myself becoming an important part of society."

Typical adolescent identity struggles, you say? Predictable teenage mood swings? Maybe. And perhaps I could write them off as such . . . if I wasn't a professional family

"For many of us, erosion of self-worth began in childhood."

counselor . . . if I didn't see the pattern repeated a thousand times in a thousand ways. In preteens and businesswomen . . . in high-flying executive types and homemakers . . . in grandmothers and grandfathers . . . in pastors and millionaires.

Self-hate. Acute negativism. Anger turned inward.

Many of these same people are desperately groping to establish—or salvage—vital personal relationships in their lives. They are genuinely trying to reach out. But they're having a hard time of it, and as their counselor, I'm having a hard time helping them. The reason for this struggle is simple: *The starting point for all good relationships begins by accepting and liking who I am.*

Where Does the Anger Begin?

Why is it that people tend to focus their anger inward and put themselves down? When it comes to people I love to hate, why am I usually first in line? For that matter, how many people do you know who have a genuine appreciation for their own personal strength, and at the same time a healthy acceptance of their limitations? If you're like most of us, you could invite the whole bunch over for dinner, call out for a small pizza, and have leftovers for a week.

How do these feelings get started?

For many of us, an erosion of self-worth began in childhood. Do you recall any statements like these from your earlier years? "Mother won't like you if you don't get your room cleaned . . ." "Why don't you get good grades like your brother does . . ." "If you would just *try*, you could get straight A's . . ." "An athlete with your talent will probably get lots of scholarship offers . . ." "Do a good job when you wash the car so you don't disappoint your father. . . ."

"If I don't like myself, how can anyone else like me?"

What's the real message behind these statements? If you hear and believe enough of them, what's the bottom line? Isn't it something like this? "If I do well, I'm okay. If I mess up by doing poorly, I'm no good."

Then the thoughts spiral on downward: "If I'm no good, I can't like myself. And if I don't like myself, how can anyone else like me?"

By the time I reach the bottom, I'm not very likeable. Who wants to build a friendship with an unhappy person who has only negative feelings about herself or himself? And then when the friends don't come . . . ah, there's further evidence. "I'm not likeable. Never have been, never will be." And another step is taken down that winding path of loneliness and hurt.

When you've lived with this painful sense of personal devaluation long enough, it seems as if there is nothing you can do that's worthy of praise. No matter how well you do, it's not good enough. Someone compliments you and instead of saying "Thank you," you look for a way to put yourself down.

I remember following a confrontive, older lady out of church several years ago. As she shook the pastor's hand she said, "Thank you for that sermon today. It was good."

The pastor responded, "Don't thank me, just thank the Lord."

Without blinking an eye the woman retorted, "I didn't say it was *that* good."

What happened in that interchange? There was a lady who was seeking to encourage her pastor. But the pastor may have had difficulty accepting credit for a job well done. When he refused to accept the compliment, the lady added an insult. I think it was her way of saying, "If you insist on putting yourself down . . . if you can't accept a word of sincere appreciation . . . then let me on the bandwagon. I'll put you down, too."

It is, however, a lonely feeling to think you can't do anything right. And it's even worse when you believe that people won't like you unless you "perform" well. When you're immersed in that kind of thinking, life seems to lose direction and meaning. Long before that, it loses joy.

Where Self-Acceptance Can Enter In

Let's move back to the starting point of all good relationships: accepting and liking who I am. A cure-all for you, and for those close to you? No . . . but it is a beginning.

The process starts by asking a question something like this: Is it possible to separate who I am from what I do? That's a tough one, isn't it? And a difficult assignment at best. One certainty, however, is that the order I give to *being* (who I am) and *doing* (what I do) is vitally important. Doing does not determine being. What I do is not what gives me worth as a person. Doing flows from being. Who I am evidences itself in what I do. My value—catch this—does not depend on what I do, good or bad.

That's a strong statement. Is it really true? How can that be possible when the Bible describes the human heart as "deceitful . . . and desperately wicked" (Jeremiah 17:9 KJV). So I do rotten things. Does that mean I'm no good or that I'm not loveable? When I mess up am I worth . . . less?

Does God love people only when they do good? The New Testament tells us: "But God demonstrates his own love for us in this: While we were still sinners, Christ died for us" (Romans 5:8). Redeeming love reached beyond what we do to save who we are.

But does this mean God doesn't care what we do? Of course not. He is vitally interested. Solomon put it succinctly when he said, "For a man's ways are in full view of the LORD, and he examines all his paths" (Proverbs 5:21). God doesn't like it when we engage in hurtful activities, and He calls it for what it is—sin. He rejoices when we are obedient to His commands. But He loves us *regardless*. Nothing has the ability to separate us from God's love:

> "For I am convinced that neither death nor life, neither angels nor demons, neither the present nor the future, nor any powers, neither height nor depth, nor anything else in all creation, will be able to separate us from the love of God that is in

"Is it possible to separate who I am from what I do?"

"God chooses to love me, independent of my actions."

Christ Jesus our Lord" (Romans 8:38-39).

God is able to separate who we are from what we do, and when He looks at who we are He says to each one of us: "I love you." Since God chooses to love me, independent of my actions, I know beyond all doubt that I am seen as worthy. Worthy to be loved. I am loveable.

But let's make it practical. A man leaves his marriage and lives with another woman. His wife feels discarded and angry. After several months, the husband leaves the other woman and seeks reconciliation with his wife. How should this man feel about himself, at the present moment?

Should he occupy his thoughts with, "I'm no good. I'm utterly worthless. My wife cannot by any stretch of the imagination love me after what I've done."

Or is it possible to separate his *value* from his *act*? Perhaps his thoughts could run like this: "I've done a despicable act. I've broken a commitment. I've sinned against God and against my wife. I've sought and found God's forgiveness, but now I need to tell her how wrong it was for me to do this. Since she loves me, she may find it in her heart to forgive me, and to accept me back, and to treat me as though it never happened. She loves me because I'm loveable—even when I behave in ways that hurt her and me."

Are either one of those scenarios possible? Yes, both. And I've seen both happen again and again. One path leads to bitterness, deeper hurt, and loneliness. Perhaps to suicide. The other path, though not without hurt, leads to healing, restoration, wholeness.

The first task in building better relationships is to accept and like who I am. I may despise what I do, but that does not detract from my value.

The following simple statements have helped many counselees gain needed focus. Let them help you to remember your essential worth:

1. I am loved by God—deeply and unconditionally.

2. My being (who I am) comes before my doing (what I do).

3. I can accept myself—both my areas of strength and the areas where I am less strong.

4. It is okay to let other people know who I am, for my feeling of worth is not dependent upon their approval of me.

5. Fulfillment is not to be equated with achievement.

Learning from Aloneness

Here's an irony for you: Spending time alone can help us to be less lonely. Time invested in this way may provide some revealing glimpses into who we really are.

For a lot of people, that's not a very comfortable idea. There is apprehension.

"What if I get alone with myself and find that I really don't like me? What if I discover some unpleasant things about myself ?"

The fear of such discoveries may keep us from finding times of aloneness, times of quiet. It seems less threatening somehow to deny our intrinsic value, to cling to the idea that we're not really worth knowing, to really believe that getting alone with ourselves can only be boring or disappointing.

And yet consider something. The great paradox of life is that basically we *are* alone. But we allow distractions to create the illusion that we are not. Refusing to face our aloneness, to admit to it, we end up feeling that life is little more than a "performance," carefully orchestrated to meet the expectations of others. One long charade.

And here again is the irony. We can actually decrease our feelings of loneliness by spending time alone.

For all its value, however, aloneness doesn't come easy.

A thousand distractions loom as barriers in the way. Busy schedules, television, the demands of children, escapist fiction, and the ceaseless crooning of easy-listening music (or the shattering strains of rock) can keep us from that goal. Even unselfish commitments to multiplied "worthy causes" or "ministries" crowd out opportunities to recognize and celebrate that vital inner worth which gives life purpose and direction.

We grip so tightly to the security of our many activities and duties that it seems impossible to simply relax and let the busy-ness go for a time.

The psalmist says it in this admonition:

"Be still, and know that I am God" (Psalm 46:10).

Another translation renders that first phrase "Cease striving." A literal translation of the Hebrew text might phrase it "Let go" or "Release your grip."

However you might say it, it simply isn't easy to do.

Chuck Swindoll, in his book *Standing Out*, agrees:

"For all its value, aloneness doesn't come easy."

> I visited a small town during a recent trip through central Oregon. It was one of those places that was so relaxed I found myself getting antsy. Life moves along there about the speed of a glacier. You know . . . the type of town where people gather to watch the hubcaps rust. I asked my friend: "How do you stand it? Doesn't the slow pace drive you crazy?" He responded with a smile. "Well, it took us about eight months to unwind. You gotta *learn* how to relax, Chuck. It isn't something that you do automatically. Now, we love it."

Cease striving! Let go! *Be still.* As difficult as this may be, it is necessary if I am going to accept and like who I am. "In quietness and trust," wrote the prophet, "is your strength" (Isaiah 30:15).

When I let go of the merry-go-round of scheduled activities for a while and seek out that place of quietness to reflect on myself, I begin to see that my human dignity has its

"As I come to know, value, and trust myself, I will be enabled to extend that trust and love to those around me."

roots in the Person of God. I learn how to experience myself in non-judgmental ways—to hear, to feel, and to touch with deepened sensitivity.

With time, the view of myself develops until I can see what it means to respect myself for who I am, both my strengths and my limitations. I am a valuable human being who has feelings, who can experience life in its fullness—with all its pain, love, beauty, and sorrow. As I come to know, value, and trust myself, I will be enabled to extend that trust and love to those around me.

Two Ways to Treat Yourself

Contrast Moses and Jesus. If any man qualified for the title of "loser," it was the youthful Moses. Why? He began his career in winning form. Raised as an heir to the throne of Pharaoh in an Egypt that was at the crest of world power, culture, and learning, Moses was "Mr. Everything." Prestigious education, refined upbringing, limitless wealth, stellar future . . . I can't imagine this adopted son of royalty having any problems lining up dates for Friday night.

Moses, however, was a Jew, not an Egyptian. Seeing one of his enslaved countrymen suffering abuse at the hands of an Egyptian taskmaster, Moses simply walked over and killed the oppressor. Misunderstood by both Jew and Egyptian, this once ever-so-promising young man fled to a wilderness in Midian. He signed on at a sheep ranch and prepared for what he thought would surely be a life of obscurity.

At this point the former prince must have felt rotten. He had failed, missed his opportunity, done poorly, let everyone down. He was no good. . . . Can't you just hear those thoughts and feel those feelings?

Forty years later, however, God appeared to Moses. Now eighty years old, this adoptive son of royalty was still tending sheep for his father-in-law/employer. At this seemingly inauspicious juncture of Moses' life, God commissioned him to return to Egypt and lead the Hebrew people out of slavery and into a land of promise.

It was one of the most important, highly responsible tasks God ever gave anyone. Ever. And Moses had trouble handling the idea. What do you suppose went through his mind as he knelt before that burning bush in the desert?

"I tried to do that forty years ago. All it got me was hatred from the Egyptians, an undying indifference from the Israelites, and a one-way, last-class ticket to Midian. I was younger then, had a decent set of threads, and the keys to Egypt's Air Force One. Now I'm an old man, and God says He wants me. . . ."

Those words may not express exactly how Moses felt, but he did put himself down, didn't he? He offered one excuse after another. Exodus chapters 3 and 4 record how he rattled them off, one by one: "I'm a nobody. Who will I say sent me? What if they don't believe me? I'm not a good speaker. My brother's better than I. . . ."

"I tried to do that forty years ago . . . all it got me was a one-way last-class ticket to Midian."

"Can you think of one incident where Jesus put Himself down?"

Moses, it seems, had never learned to accept who he was and to like that person. Even when the Almighty God actually appeared to him and promised to be his help and strength and Companion, it wasn't enough. "O Lord," he said, "please send someone else."

Now contrast this scene with the life of Jesus. Many people like to create a picture of Jesus as an unobtrusive, non-assertive person. But that's not true. Can you think of one incident where Jesus put Himself down? His life on earth was amazing.

How did Jesus feel about Himself: Did He accept who He was? Did He like Himself?

The more I study the earthly walk of Christ, the more I become convinced that self-awareness and self-acceptance were keys to His life. His outward expressions of love and inner manifestations of mental health provide a sterling example of what life can be. Read through the gospels and you see a Man who was in control of every situation He encountered.

He never apologized for Who He was. He was not intimidated by people. He refused to cater to people's expectations. At age twelve he boldly confronted the religious leaders in the temple. One of the last pictures of Jesus prior to the crucifixion is when He washed the feet of His followers. Instead of sliding into a secure, predictable mold, He continually startled everyone who knew Him. They simply could not forecast what this astonishing Man would do or say next.

Jesus was a rule-breaker. In word and

deed, He attacked the restrictive legalism of the religious leaders of the first century. By healing broken bodies on the Sabbath, He turned His back on the traditions of the synagogue. Instead of cowering before the stern-faced Pharisees, He called them hypocrites and phonies. And worse. To their faces. He accused them of trying to pick a bit of sawdust out of a person's eye when they had half a log crammed under their own eyelids.

Jesus appeared to have no need to defend Himself. He just declared Himself. His life is a model of tolerance, confrontiveness, and self-disclosure. Jesus knew who He was, accepted who He was, ánd received love—as He was.

"Jesus appeared to have no need to defend Himself. He just declared Himself."

As It Was with Him—So It Can Be with Us

My worth does not depend on what I do, good or bad, professional or amateur, consistent or sporadic, organized and put-together or impulsive and spontaneous. But I must begin by accepting and liking who I am. The evidence of healthy self-esteem in my life will be found in a willingness to declare, openly and without apology, who I am. This will provide other people with an opportunity to know me and to decide if they want to build a relationship with me.

Isn't that where it begins? I seek out people I want to know better. They, in turn, respond in a positive way and we establish a foundation for a meaningful relationship. Or, happily, people seek me out because they find me likeable. They communicate an interest in me. I respond and a friendship begins.

People like me because they see me as worthwhile to them. How do I know? I know because I've accepted who I am. I like myself.

◆ Interaction ◆

Set aside from one to four hours to spend time alone. Find a suitable setting, free from distraction, perhaps outside on a hillside or by a lake. While you are by yourself, mull over these questions in your mind:

1. In what ways have I added to my stress by focusing on others instead of myself?

2. What distractions have kept me from looking at my own value and from setting future directions for myself?

3. How can I recognize and understand more deeply my relationship to God?

4. What are some of the qualities that I admire in myself?

5. Who are three people I would most like to build a deeper relationship with during the next six months?

When you return from your time alone, find a notebook and start a journal. Enter your reflective thoughts. Keep the journal

where it is readily accessible so that you can
enter more ideas or go back to read things
previously entered.

- Avoid Withdrawing ▰▰▰▰▰
  - Avoid Placating ════════
    - Avoid Intruding ════════

    - Learn Giving ════════════
    - Learn Receiving ══════════
  - Learn Inviting ════════════
- Learn Contributing ══════════

Chapter 2

Avoid Withdrawing
—Face the Option of Risk—

BEFORE I DEAL with the issue of withdrawal, I want to set forth a question which will frame the rest of the book for you.

I've encountered the question a thousand times, though not always in so many words. Sometimes people can't seem to verbalize it, and yet they want the answer more than a million dollar lottery ticket. I've seen it asked most eloquently by pleading eyes looking at me from lonely faces. I've heard it echoed in sad stories of personal struggle and dreams that cling for life on the cliff edge of despair.

It's a question I've asked myself again and again. And maybe I've been discovering some satisfactory answers.

The question is simply this: *Are there a few principles I can apply to help me build better relationships?*

Searching for answers to that query, I've

looked for guidelines that are both economical and comprehensive.

By *economical*, I mean that I don't want to have any more principles than I really need. I want to keep the number small. Easy to remember.

By *comprehensive*, I mean, "This will do it; this is enough." If I follow these guidelines I will have the minimum essentials for building healthy relationships.

The principles themselves are simple enough to memorize in a minute or two. But to really learn them? To achieve them? It could take hours and weeks and years of hard work—and generous portions of God's grace.

The list is divided into two sections: things I need to avoid and things I need to learn. Let's take a look at the key words now, and then look more carefully at each through the pages of this book.

- Avoid Withdrawing
- Avoid Placating
- Avoid Intruding
- Learn Giving
- Learn Receiving
- Learn Inviting
- Learn Contributing

To build better relationships, I must really apply myself to all seven principles. If I faithfully adhere to six, neglecting even one of these guidelines, chances are good my relationships will be less rewarding than I want them to be.

Work with me in these next pages, first to

understand the guideline or principle, and then to seek ways to apply this idea to your own relationships.

We'll begin with that first big "AVOID."

Withdrawal: The Peril and the Pain

"Withdrawal" is a term counselors and psychologists like to use. But perhaps you've used some different words for it . . . such as "the silent treatment."

Does that call up a painful memory or two? Forgetting for a moment about the times when you've used that kind of behavior (you have to admit it, don't you?), can you recall what it felt like to be on the receiving end of that wall-like silence?

Frustrated? Hurt? Angry? Discouraged? Wondering what in the world you did wrong or what you could possibly do to make things better?

It's not pleasant when all of a sudden the boss stops talking to you . . . or your friend always seems to be "in a hurry" when you try to make conversation . . . or your dad has been ignoring you.

The deepest, most disruptive pain of all may be withdrawal in a marriage relationship. Here are two people who have pledged before God to become one—to share their very lives with each other. And now one partner begins to pull back. It may be a mental withdrawal, a physical withdrawal, or both. The resulting emotions of helpless hurt and frustration are verbalized many ways in the counseling office, but the sad, underlying

". . . can you recall what it felt like to be on the receiving end of wall-like silence?"

"Our lives have grown apart somehow."

tone is the same.

"My husband doesn't seem interested in sex anymore. What's wrong?"

"My wife has become so quiet lately, almost aloof. It used to be that she couldn't wait to see me after work. We talked about all kinds of things—the kids, work, weekend plans, friends, relatives. You name it, we talked about it. But now . . . all I get is this peck on the cheek with a half-hearted 'Hello.' These deathly silent evenings, just staring at a book or watching TV, they're getting to me."

"Our lives have grown apart somehow. He spends more and more time away from home. If he's not at work, then he's with friends or doing things by himself. We don't seem to have time for each other any more."

These statements are expressions of pain. The spouse is hurting over a mate's decision to withdraw, to quit investing in the relationship. One partner has simply locked the other partner out. Such an action can cause as much pain as a spouse who physically packs up and walks out the door.

Sometimes these "silent periods" are short-lived or sporadic things. At other times they are much longer, and much more devastating.

I think of George and Linda on that first day they came for counseling. What a graphic example. Linda was the one being "walled out," and before she had spoken a half dozen words, the fragile thread holding in her emotions gave way in a torrent of tears. It seemed as if her once-desired dreams were floating away like pieces of wreckage in that bitter flood.

George was considering a divorce. Another woman. He'd fallen hard for Vivian, and he could no longer keep it from his wife.

It wasn't a pretty picture. George sat sullen and still while his wife cried harder and harder. Withdrawn? I had the distinct feeling that George was so emotionally withdrawn that knocking him over the head with a tire iron wouldn't have brought a reaction out of him.

What a dreadful situation. Eleven years of marriage crumbling before my eyes like a charred cardboard box. There were no band-aids that could heal those wounds. No quick fixes. Heavyhearted, I longed for sensitivity and wisdom. This troubled man, this heartbroken woman were trying to bring me into their anguished world. Was healing possible?

The bridge of communication between Linda and George, after some years of damaging erosion, had taken a direct hit. A canyon of pain now stretched between them. George had chosen to withdraw, to isolate himself, his thoughts, and his feelings from his wife. On her side, Linda was frantically trying to find ways to rebuild the bridge. But it would require time, willingness, commitment, and *hard work* from all three of us. I was ready for the task. But were they?

The example I've just related was from a marriage relationship—and a rather extreme situation at that. But the thought

"Withdrawal in a friendship or marriage carries with it the potential for damage and destruction."

". . . you and I both tend to store up hurts inside of us, and they don't usually go away with time."

behind it holds true for *any* relationship at *any* level. Withdrawal in a friendship or marriage carries with it the potential for damage and destruction. Dealing with it requires discipline, effort, and courage. But it must be dealt with if a relationship is to develop or grow!

Facing Up to My Withdrawal

It can be stated as simply as this: When something happens that could hurt my relationship with a friend, I need to do my part to resolve the situation. It is dangerous to shrug it off with a self-assuring comment such as: "Well, if I back off things will get better with time. I really don't need to do anything." That kind of thinking can be the first wrong turn in a whole series of tragic wrong turns. The truth is that you and I both tend to store up hurts inside of us, and they don't usually go away with time. Instead, they may fester, turning affection or love into bitterness.

The Bible says, "If you are angry, don't sin by nursing your grudge. Don't let the sun go down with you still angry—get over it quickly" (Ephesians 4:26, TLB).

Have you found yourself in the position of trying again and again to patch up a faltering relationship?

While it only seems natural to retreat when you've been hurt—perhaps many times—we must face the fact that relationships can never be formed, developed, or maintained while you're retreating! You can't reach out and run backwards at the same time. You must either take the risk and expend the effort (for the thousandth time?) or let the relationship go. There is really no "middle ground."

Withdrawal must also be dealt with before a relationship ever begins. Think of a person you've observed for some time, someone you'd really like to get to know. Someone you'd like to be friends with. (It doesn't have to be a romantic situation. If you're married, it might be another couple you and your spouse would like to draw close to.)

There is a troublesome tendency in that situation to hesitate, to withdraw from making that first contact. A hundred "What-ifs?" come to mind which could keep the relationship from developing. These thoughts are often strengthened by painful memories of past efforts that didn't go well. The strangling apprehension of possible rejection can drive us into a corner of inactivity . . . and loneliness.

Perhaps it's just a matter of that first step, that first word, that first motion in the other person's direction. "Other people," you complain to yourself, "seem to talk so easily. It doesn't appear to bother them at all to go up to a complete stranger and start a conversation. I could *never* do that."

And you're probably right. Not immediately, anyway. That kind of communicative ability isn't going to be learned overnight. But if you'd like to work on it, here are some suggestions which may encourage you to make a beginning:

"The strangling apprehension of possible rejection can drive us into a corner of inactivity . . . and loneliness."

1. When you do find the opportunity to start a conversation, don't overdo it! Don't talk too much. Short periods of silence may feel awkward, but will not necessarily keep a relationship from progressing.

2. Learn to listen and ask questions that provide opportunities for the other person to expand on what he or she is saying.

3. Take the responsibility for *finishing* the conversation before it starts to lag. Try to leave the person with the feeling that you both have lots more to say next time there is opportunity to talk.

It requires effort on my part if I want to build a new relationship. It requires effort on my part to mend a faltering relationship. I may, of course, choose to withdraw rather than extend that kind of effort. By doing so, I avoid the possibility of being hurt. At the same time, however, the relationships I want and need will continue to elude my grasp. I will exchange the risk of rejection for the empty ache of loneliness.

When Pulling Back Is an Option

It would be nice if these guidelines could be stated, explained, and followed to improved relationships—every time. It would be nice; but it wouldn't be realistic. Unfortunately, life is more complicated than that. Each of the guidelines in building a relationship needs to be carefully considered in terms of your unique, individual situation. They are, after all, *guidelines.* Helpful principles. Suggestions that generally apply.

But there are exceptions, even in this matter of withdrawal. Pulling back is not always negative. It may, in fact, be necessary.

If you have a disagreement with your spouse or a friend and you find that you are both becoming more emotional than logical, it might be wise to say something like this:

"Look . . . I'm not hearing what you're trying to say to me, and I'm having difficulty getting my viewpoint across to you. Could we talk about this again tomorrow? In the meantime, I'll think about what you've said and try to find ways to clarify my thoughts when I talk to you."

The hurt and embarrassment of a loud argument (particularly when it happens around other people) can be avoided by temporarily withdrawing when you see a disagreement beginning to "boil over."

But let me stress the word "temporarily" again. The relationship cannot grow while you are withdrawn. There needs to be a coming together and a resolution of the disagreement that brought out the anger.

There are other instances when permanent withdrawal is the only wise option. Not all relationships are healthy, or in our best interests. In those instances withdrawal, in spite of the possible hurt feelings and difficult consequences, is a vital and necessary "emergency exit."

You could talk to Joseph about that. Genesis 39 relates an unforgettable

"Pulling back is not always negative."

*"You can-
not control
what some-
one else
chooses to
do."*

"withdrawal." Sold into slavery in Egypt, the handsome young son of Jacob found himself elevated to a position of responsibility in the house of Potiphar, captain of Pharaoh's elite guard. A godly, reliable young man, Joseph eventually was set over the military man's whole household. All went well until Potiphar's love-hungry wife began trying to seduce the Israelite. Bold and brazen as they come, the woman tried again and again to corner Joseph, who may have been hardly more than a teenager. "Come to bed with me!" she crooned, and used all her wiles to make that prospect very, very attractive.

Joseph resisted and resisted. But then she caught up with him when they were alone in the house. Not willing to be denied her fantasy, she gripped the young man by his cloak and pushed her proposition—hard.

Scripture says, "he left his cloak in her hand and ran out of the house" (Genesis 39:12). Joseph knew that the time for reasoning and logic was past. *He ran.* And even though the consequences of his action were difficult, later events would show that a hasty withdrawal was the very best decision he could have made.

Facing Up to Another's Withdrawal

Another side of this question could be phrased in this way: "What can I do if my friend (or spouse) chooses to withdraw from me?"

We'll be looking carefully at some specific options later in this book—in the "Learn" portion of the guidelines. But we must keep one crucial truth in focus: *You cannot control what someone else chooses to do.*

It goes back to the request I made at the very beginning of the book. Remember the two things I asked you to do? (1) Look ahead, and (2) focus on yourself.

If someone very dear to you chooses to withdraw or to leave you, there are times when all you can do is to let them go. The specter of death is always beyond our control. Divorce can be. Broken engagements and dating relationships can leave us helpless as well. The closer and deeper the relationship, the harder it is to accept the reality of a situation and to unclench those fingers . . . and release.

At such times of sorrow and hurt, it is good, like the cold, sweet water from a deep well, to reflect on a relationship that shall not, *cannot* fail. Let your mind linger on that three and a half years Jesus spent with His disciples. What a friendship they developed. The exultant moments of triumph and the heat of opposition and danger drew them closer than brothers. The disciples had left their jobs—the only life they knew—to follow in His path. They loved this unusual Galilean, and how He loved them!

Then there was that last, bittersweet meal before their Friend faced the cross. He spoke words that wrenched their souls: He would be taken from them, rejected by them, humiliated, beaten, killed. But He spoke soothing words as well: He would be raised to life; death could not separate them; He

"I may withdraw from Him. And yet He waits patiently for me to return."

would send His Spirit to guide and comfort
them; and though physically absent from
their midst, He would never leave nor abandon them.

It's a picture I have of God as I write these
words. He is the One who seeks a relationship with me, through His Son, Jesus Christ.
And once that relationship has been established He has chosen *never* to withdraw from
me.

I may withdraw from Him. And yet He
waits patiently for me to return. His arms are
open. I can hear Him say, "I'm right here. I
love you. Whenever you wish to experience
My grace or mercy, it's available. I won't
push, but it's there. Just ask!"

"Let us then approach the throne of grace
with confidence, so that we may receive
mercy and find grace to help us in our time of
need" (Hebrews 4:16).

Mercy and grace. In the nick of time. Isn't
that just like Jesus?

◆ Interaction ◆

Determine one relationship you choose to
change in the next three weeks. In your journal, list five things you will stop doing and
five things you will start doing to effect that
change.

At the end of three weeks, write a response
in your journal in terms of how you feel
about the relationship now as opposed to
when you started three weeks earlier.

• Avoid Withdrawing ▰▰▰▰▰▰▰▰
  ● **Avoid Placating** ▰▰▰▰▰▰▰▰
   • Avoid Intruding ═══════════

    • Learn Giving ═══════════
    • Learn Receiving ═══════════
   • Learn Inviting ═══════════
• Learn Contributing ═══════════

Chapter 3

Avoid Placating
—Wean Yourself from the Expectations of Others—

WHY DO I DO WHAT I DO?

Talk about a tough question. People have been throwing that one around for a long time. Nearly two millenia ago a fellow named Paul was wrestling with that very issue in his letter to the Romans.

Perhaps you've heard that question answered in this way:

"I did what I did because it was expected of me. That's what I thought people wanted me to do."

Do you go along with that line of thought? Do we build better relationships by gearing our behavior to meet other people's expectations?

I used to think that. I really did. But I've changed my mind.

Let's consider a hypothetical (but maybe close to home?) illustration.

The Saga of George and Samantha

Samantha Sludge has trouble making up her mind. About anything. George Goosebump, by contrast, has such a take-charge orientation he'd make a five-star general blush. If you put them together, what kind of relationship do you suppose will develop? A good one? You might think so—at first. Since Samantha dislikes the responsibility of making decisions and George loves to decide for anybody, it would appear that their compatibility would approach the fabled dietary harmony of Jack and Mrs. Spratt.

> Jack Spratt could eat no fat,
>   His wife could eat no lean,
> And so between the two of them,
>   They licked the platter clean.

Ask Samantha a question. Her favorite response, not surprisingly, is "I dunno." George, however, has an opinion on any topic. From apoplexy to Zen, or from avocado cultivation to zoological innovation, George has it covered—and will let you know it.

Now put this couple at a party and ask them a question. George answers. Samantha smiles. On the surface it looks okay, maybe even good. But take a closer look. The relationship isn't healthy.

Why, you ask? Because Samantha isn't a *person*. She's what she thinks George wants her to be. Since she has never developed the skill of decision-making, her life is less than it could be. She is diminished.

I can't be dogmatic on this point. There are some similar relationships between dictator and placator that seem to be doing okay. If both people in the relationship want this sort of arrangement and work diligently to "do their part," a certain level of comfort and predictability may develop, such as is found in ill-fitting shoes that are finally stretched out and worn down. And even though such an arrangement may be "acceptable" to the people involved, it is still anemic and unhealthy.

"Do what you do because you choose to do it."

A Better Alternative

Do what you do because you choose to do it.
Do those words seem startling? Do they strike you as selfish? Let me suggest another one-word description of the concept: authentic. Those who subscribe to this alternative may not find their behaviors changing much at all in given situations. But their motives? That's a very different matter.

I may, for instance, choose to buy a birthday gift for my friend because I want to communicate how special this person is to me. On the other hand, I could go out and buy the same gift and present it with the same smile because I feel he or she "expects" me to. I really don't want to buy anything. I can't afford it right now . . . but I want that person to continue liking me.

Do you see the distinction? If I do something just because I feel someone *expects* me to, then I am likely to resent what I'm doing. But if I do it because I really *want* to do it,

"If I out-wardly agree with someone, but inwardly disagree, I am sowing seeds of resentment in the relationship."

then I can accept full responsibility for my action.

This means that at times I will have to disagree with people, even at the risk of offending them. I will have to confront people, as graciously and tactfully as I can, with thoughts and statements that may cause them to back up a step or two. Why do I do this? Because if I outwardly agree with someone, *but inwardly disagree,* I am sowing seeds of resentment in the relationship. Those seeds can grow into ugly seedlings, and then become poisonous, destructive plants. In other words, "faking it" or placating the other person to smooth over an awkward moment may be more destructive in the long run than by simply being honest—even at the risk of embarrassment or offense.

Put yourself in the position of a young woman whose date wants to express affection with a kiss. Very honestly, she doesn't want that expression. She isn't ready for it, the relationship isn't ready for it; she would be much happier and feel a lot better if he refrained. But she likes this guy. The friendship seems to have some potential. Should she "go along" with his physical advances in order to preserve the relationship and not offend him?

She could. But if she continues to placate, building up inner resentments, the relationship is as good as finished anyway. She will not only lose respect for her boyfriend, she'll lose respect for herself.

"Serve" Does Not Mean "Placate"

In addition to the struggles we've been talking about, Christians have to wrestle with New Testament concepts such as "being a servant" and "submitting to one another."

Look at the life of Christ Jesus. Wasn't He a servant? "The Son of Man," He told us, "did not come to be served, but to serve, and to give his life as a ransom for many" (Mark 10:45). This is where a distinction becomes crucial: Jesus was a servant. He was not a placator. His whole life on earth was invested in ministry to people, yet the One who called Himself the Son of Man did not reach out or heal or speak or love or sacrifice because someone expected Him to. He never acted in order to win affection or approval or kindly smiles and nods of the head.

Jesus did what He did because He chose to do it! He obeyed His Father because it was the desire of His heart. He acted volitionally. He spoke sharp words because they needed to be spoken, even at the risk of alienating His best friends and arousing the wrath of the authorities.

He was, every moment of His life, Himself. He was a servant because He chose that role, not because He "wanted to please." He lived a life of self-sacrifice, meeting needs, washing feet, and giving Himself over to a Roman death machine because it was in His heart to do so.

That is servanthood. That is not placating.

"Jesus was a servant. He was not a placator."

*"I can no
more de-
mand sub-
mission
from my
wife than
you can
demand a
servant's
heart from
me."*

"Submit" Does Not Mean "Placate"

The book of Ephesians surfaces yet another question mark in many minds. Husbands, the apostle affirms, are to love their wives, and wives are to submit to their husbands (Ephesians 5:25, 22).

Viewpoints, interpretations, and personal biases run rampant on this passage. Almost everywhere you turn you can hear someone explaining, or explaining away, this Scripture. But the fact is, if you want a good marriage, the principles ring out as clearly as the day Paul first stated them:

> Husbands, love your wives. Wives, submit to your husbands.

Submit, however, does not mean *placate*.

Submitting is a personal response to a specific scriptural directive. It is a matter of the heart between the One who said it, God, and the one who must choose whether to obey that or not obey that, the wife.

It is not for the husband to dictate. Scripture has a word for him: *love*. Period. I can no more demand submission from my wife than you, my fellow Christian, can demand a servant's heart from me. My servant's heart is between the Lord and me. If I have one, it is because I have chosen to follow Christ in this matter. If I do not, then He is the One to whom I will answer.

Submission that is mere outward compliance in order to placate a dictator will not insure a good relationship. It may, in fact, destroy it. And the husband who chooses to press this point may end up winning a slave . . . and losing a friend and companion.

Frankly, I get irritated when husbands come to me and say, "The problem in our marriage is that my wife isn't submissive."

"Garbage," I reply. "The problem in your marriage is that you are focusing on your wife's behavior rather than your own."

"Negotiate" Does Not Mean "Placate"

Do what you do, we've been saying, because you choose to do it. Placating, or giving in, is damaging to relationships and should be avoided.

But what kind of world would this be if everyone took this advice? Wouldn't it excuse a lot of belligerence? Think, for instance, of the wife who asks her husband to go shopping with her. He could set his shoulders and say, "Forget it! It's raining and dark outside, I'm comfortable in my recliner, and I'm not giving in to you."

Sure, the man has avoided placating. But he's also hurt his wife's feelings and has probably won for himself an evening of miserable silence. Instead of acting so belligerently, he would probably find life more tolerable if he practiced some *negotiation*. "I'm not really anxious to put on my raincoat and go shopping," he might say, "but I would like to have the Smiths over tomorrow night. If you'll stop by the deli with me to get some cheese and chips, I'll go with you to get the stuff you want to buy."

Has he "given in"? Not really. He has

"... placating seeks to 'buy' friendship ... a technique that simply doesn't work."

negotiated with his wife. People, after all, are traders. Most of us will give something if we get something in return. The storybook youngster named Jack might have had such a barter system in mind when he traded his cow. "I'll give you Daisy here for that bag of magic beans . . . if in the end I get a goose that lays golden eggs."

Don't confuse negotiation with placation. There are times when I may choose to do something I *don't* want to do because by doing it I can gain something I *do* want. Negotiation has the implied aspect of getting something out of the transaction that is meaningful and rewarding to me. Placating, on the other hand, is the effort to get people to like me by doing what I think they want me to do. In a sense, placating seeks to "buy" friendship. It is a technique that simply doesn't work.

Placating Can't Buy Friendships

I can remember trying to "purchase" friendship as a teenager. If I used my parents' car to take my buddies where they wanted to go . . . and if I spent my own money to buy us all milkshakes now and then . . . maybe the guys would accept me and like to have me around. My bribes, of course, didn't win me the friends I wanted so deeply. I'd hoped to get something out of the transaction that was meaningful and rewarding, but it didn't happen.

At other times we're tempted to placate just to get some relief. That other person is pushing and pushing; he or she won't let up or take no for an answer. So you say, "Okay, okay," and you give in just to get that individual off your back. Once again, however, the strategy doesn't work! The more you give in, the more the other person wants and the more you resent that individual. So instead of a growing relationship, you find yourself with growing bitterness.

It doesn't have to be that way. Choosing your own direction is not only a personal privilege; it's a God-given responsibility.

> *"Choosing your own direction is not only a personal privilege; it's a God-given responsibility."*

Who's Holding the Wheel?

This whole matter of choosing my own direction in life, without trying to placate, takes me back (again) to some vivid scenes from my teenage years. Some of you are much closer to those years than I am, but the memories . . . well, they can still make me smile. Or sigh. Or shudder in disbelief!

Have you ever played "chicken"? I don't recommend it. It's one of the most foolhardy games I can think of, right alongside Russian roulette. The rules for the version my friends and I used to play were simple: Everyone got into the car and the driver accelerated down the road. At a given signal the driver would let go of the steering wheel. The first person to panic and grab the wheel was "chicken." That individual was the loser, or so I used to think.

Fortunately for me, there was always someone in the car who didn't have to prove his or her bravery, someone with the good sense to grab the wheel before an accident occurred.

Today I'm older, and, I hope, wiser. I don't want to play "chicken" with my life anymore. By that I mean I want to steer my own life, choose my own direction, make my own decisions.

That seems to run counter to some of the advice you and I received as we've faced difficult questions and decisions.

"Just trust God," we've been told. "He'll tell you what to do." Or "Let go . . . and let God."

Is that what God wants, for me to let go of the steering wheel and trust Him to grab it before my life runs into the ditch? Does God, then, steer my life, merely allowing me along for the ride? Or . . . does He allow me to steer, furnishing me with all the resources I need to make wise decisions?

From my perspective, the latter view makes a lot more biblical sense. If God had wanted "yes-men" He could have easily created such agreeable robots. Instead, He gave us the freedom to choose. And as I choose, God doesn't want me to "placate" Him, "giving in" to Him because He's the dictator or because I want to get Him off my back. I obey Him because I choose to do so. Because loving Him and serving Him are important to me.

That's not placating.

That's love.

◆ Interaction ◆

One of the communicative skills you will want to develop is learning how to discuss something that bothers you without (1) placating the other person, or (2) assuming responsibility for the behavior of the other person.

Practice the development of this skill in a two-step process. First, determine the person and the unpleasant situation you want to discuss (e.g., a close companion fails to cover his/her mouth when he or she coughs, and you often get sprayed with what you consider to be contaminants). This is only an example. Select any bothersome or sensitive area you feel is appropriate and one you can handle.

Now choose a close friend and role play the dialogue with this person for five or ten minutes. When you have finished, ask for pointers on ways you could have done better. Specifically, ask your friend if at any point you have come across in a placating or insistent way. Ask for suggestions of other ways to say the same things and still maintain your primary objectives.

Second, try it out on the person whose behavior has bothered you. Talk enough with the individual to make sure the person knows how you feel. When you have finished, write a paragraph in your personal journal evaluating the experience.

Now repeat this exercise, expressing the *positive* feelings you have over something you

like about the other person's behavior. Keep
the same guidelines. As you practice this interaction exercise, you will gain confidence
in expressing both your positive and negative feelings.

- Avoid Withdrawing ▰▰▰▰▰◣
  - Avoid Placating ▰▰▰▰▰◣
    - ● Avoid Intruding ▰▰▰▰▰◣

    - Learn Giving ══════════
    - Learn Receiving ════════
    - Learn Inviting ═════════
- Learn Contributing ═══════

Chapter 4

Avoid Intruding
—Wait until the Door Is Opened—

WHEN SHOULD YOU poke your nose into someone else's life and tell them what they need to do?

Perhaps that query makes you smile. You might be reflecting on times when you were either the pok*ER* or the pok*EE*. You might also be visualizing the pathetic, stereotyped busybody, always meddling, gossiping, and interfering.

Don't let those characterizations pull you away from the serious nature of this question: At what point, if there is such a point at all, do you step into someone's life with a word of counsel or warning?

"Just a Discreet Word or Two?"

For a moment imagine that you are the friend of the biblical King David. You've

"When is it appropriate to tell someone what to do?"

been watching what appears to be going on between him and Bathsheba (2 Samuel 11). You've seen David's face flush when he passes Uriah's wife in the street. Quite honestly, you're concerned about the welfare of your distracted and all-too-idle friend. What should you do?

Examining your options, you realize that you could invite the king out for lunch and warn him of how dangerously close to trouble he is treading.

Another option would be to get discreetly a quick word or two to Mrs. Uriah.

"Please, stay away from David. Go visit your sister in Kadesh-barnea for a few weeks. And by the way, they're having a sale on window curtains at Jeconiah's Department Store this week . . . a word to the wise is sufficient, ma'am."

Can you feel the pinch? On the one hand you're thinking, "It really isn't any of my business." On the other hand you're asking, "But what are true friends for if you can't help one another when it's needed?"

We're right back to our initial question: When is it appropriate to tell someone what to do? Is there any factor I can use to help me determine "when" and "if"?

"Well," you might answer, "if my motive is always to help the other person, then it's okay . . . isn't it?"

Others might respond, "You should only tell others what to do when they are members of your family."

Then again, a few will maintain, "It's never appropriate to intrude. Stay out of it!"

Listening to all of these opinions can become quite academic. But what if David turns out to be your own son, or Bathsheba your own daughter?

A Parent's Dilemma

Mothers and fathers agonize over the trials and troubles of their children. I've heard it from the lips of frustrated parents time after time:

"He just won't listen."

"She doesn't pay any attention to what we try to tell her."

All parents worthy of the name want the best for their children. It hurts so much to see a son or daughter plunge into a poor decision and pay the painful consequences. Can it really be wrong to try to help them by telling them what to do?

On the other hand, parents want their children to become independent, responsible persons. But what good are all those years of bumps, bruises, and hard-worn wisdom if you can't bring that experience to bear on your child's life now and then?

What a difficult, delicate balance! You don't want to hang on too tightly, you want to give them a little rope . . . but it can be a rotten, dangerous world. Those kids need to be warned!

And so the inner struggle rages. Sometimes, of course, that inner battle spills over into heated family "discussions." It's something that happens frequently when too many people are occupying the same space.

*"Stay out of
another
person's
space unless
and until
you've been
invited."*

The "space" I'm referring to here really
has nothing to do with how many bedrooms
or square feet your home has ... it goes
deeper than that ... and begins to answer
the question we started with: When should
you intervene in someone else's life?

Space Invasions!

When I talk about "space," I'm speaking of
that space over which you have control. It in-
cludes your feelings, thoughts, and actions.
Your space is you ... not just your tangible
body, but the you that lives and interacts with
others.

In any relationship it is possible to think of
my space, your space, and that space which
we share together—our space.

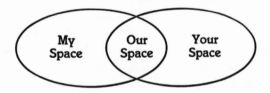

If one of the seven principles for building
better relationships is to "avoid intruding,"
then we could also state that truth in this
way: *Stay out of another person's space unless and
until you have been invited into that space.*

Permit me one small disclaimer before I go
on. In parent-child relationships, particularly in the earlier years when a child has a
limited sense of responsibility, there will obviously be times that this principle will not

apply. It finds its application between two or more mature, responsible people.

What causes one person to invade another person's space? What's the motivation? Is it just that some people derive a sense of importance from trying to run other people's lives? I don't think so.

When our own needs are not being met— when you or I hurt, feel desperate, or think a situation is unfair—the emotional pain we feel may drive us to seek need fulfillment by stepping in and trying to change the situation.

A young wife named Cindy, for instance, feels the need for affirmation and affection from her husband, Jeff. Her mate, however, is one of those easily preoccupied individuals, largely insensitive to others' needs.

He is surprised, consequently, when Cindy seems to blurt right out of the blue, "Jeff, do you *really* love me?" Cindy is not trying to be pushy, malicious, mean, or inconsiderate. Not at all. She's hurting. Something infinitely precious to her, the affection of her mate, is being withheld. By pushing her way into Jeff's space, she hopes that he will finally notice her distress and provide the attention she is craving.

How was Cindy to know that Jeff's alma mater was six points behind in the fourth quarter of the televised football game when she asked her question? And Jeff could have been a little more tactful with his reply. "Yes, I love you . . . but you're standing in front of the TV. Please move!" Cindy wonders which he likes more . . . her or his Sony.

The bottom line, however, is that Cindy's intrusions into Jeff's space didn't work! Her needs were not satisfied. Instead of affirmation, she got rejection. Her pain and self-doubt have been doubled.

When, then, is it effective to invade into another person's space? Hardly ever. Invasion, even when it is born of deep, sincere, and wholly justifiable longings, is simply not an effective path to need fulfillment. It just doesn't work! My needs are not going to be met. In fact, this sort of intrusion brings three deadly dangers into a relationship.

Danger #1: Space Invasion Creates Irresponsibility

Let me illustrate this danger from a counseling case of several years ago. Randy had brought his wife, Sarah, an admitted skeptic of the counseling process, in for an appointment. Sarah, he explained, had left him three weeks previously. And Randy wanted her back.

I turned to Sarah and asked why she had left. Randy, it seems, drank too heavily. That was part of it, but there was more. After dinner each night, it was Randy's habit to take off for "a few drinks" with his friends. That would be the last she would see or hear from him until the phone would ring sometime after midnight. The jovial voice on the other end would predictably say, "Uh . . . hiya hon . . . the guys tell me I shouldn't drive . . . ya' know? . . . Can you come get me, babe?"

Because she feared Randy couldn't handle

himself, she would awaken their seven-year-old daughter, and the two of them would "go get Daddy."

The situation might have been tolerable if it had only happened once or twice. But it had become a pattern, the usual occurrence for the last three of four years. As Sarah put it, "I've already got one kid to raise. I don't need two."

For his part, Randy had heard enough of those remarks to fill a loose-leaf binder:

"Randy, you're irresponsible."

"Randy, you're becoming as much of a bum as those bums you hang around with."

"Randy, what kind of example are you being to your daughter?"

"Randy, you're acting like a child."

"Randy, when will you grow up?"

The more obnoxious Randy's behavior became, the more Sarah would take him to task. And the more Sarah chided him, the more he would escape to the friendly confines of the tavern.

All Sarah's attempts to make her husband responsible were having exactly the opposite effect.

Danger #2: A Person May Protect His or Her Space from Invasion by Building Walls.

Picture a father who puts his arm on his teenaged son's shoulder and says, "Son, I want you to feel free to talk to me anytime. Man to man. I can remember what it was like to be your age, believe it or not, and I can also remember that I had a lot of problems. I

"Invasion . . . is simply not an effective path to need fulfillment."

"He had invited his father into his space on a very personal matter . . . Dad used the occasion to sermonize."

couldn't talk to my dad. But let's make it different with us, Son. You can talk to me about anything . . . anytime . . . okay?"

Well, that sounds good. And it isn't long before the son wonders if he should put the "open door policy" to the test. He cheated on a test in school. Should he tell Dad? After all, Dad did say, ". . . anytime . . . about anything . . ." And he really has been feeling guilty about cheating. It's been tearing at his gut for several days. So he decides to take a chance. He spills out the story to Dad.

And Dad's response? A stern, finger-shaking lecture on the values of honesty. Oh boy, that's hard to handle. The kid already felt guilty. He didn't need his dad to rub it in. But the worst part was yet to come. Now, whenever an important test was coming up in school, Dad would corner his son with an admonition: "Now remember, Son, you don't need to cheat to do well." Even after the exam at times, he would challenge him with something such as: "You didn't cheat, did you?"

One thing is for sure. Whether the son cheats or not, you can bet his dad won't find out. He had invited his father into his space on a very personal matter which had been bothering him. Instead of respecting that invitation, however, Dad used the occasion to sermonize. The result? The son who had taken the risk and responded to his father's invitation now takes his concerns and locks them up inside his own space. He is as closed to his father as if he had constructed a literal wall of brick and mortar.

Was anything wrong with the father's motivation? Not at all. He had a need to transmit to his son a system of values and integrity. Dad was just trying to do what was right. Unfortunately, his efforts backfired. Dad's needs didn't get met . . . his son's needs didn't get met . . . and now an ugly wall had come between them, all but choking off future hopes for communication.

"It's so easy to dispense a 'here's-the-formula' answer."

Danger #3: A Person May Develop an Attitude of Dependency toward the "Invader."

You don't have to be a counselor to hear comments such as these: "I feel helpless. I don't know what to do next. Tell me . . . what do you think I should do?"

We may understand that it is much better to ask careful questions of the inquirer than it is to churn out wholesale advice. We may realize that it's much better to let our friend find his own answer than it is to hand him a prepackaged one of our own. But the temptation is there . . . it's so easy to dispense a "here's the formula" answer. "I think you should" is right on the tip of our tongue.

When we do this, however, if we have reasonably good judgment and make wise decisions, this troubled person may return to us again and again . . . for more instructions; for the next step; for yet another formula. This may signal the beginning of an unhealthy dependency. Carried to an extreme, one individual in this relationship feels increasingly helpless while the other one feels increasingly exhausted!

"When people do take my advice and it turns out badly, who gets blamed? I do!"

Think about it: It takes an incredible amount of energy just to run my own life and make my own decisions. Multiply that energy drain several times and . . . watch out. An extension cord can only handle so many appliances before it begins to overheat or blows a circuit breaker.

Guess Who Gets the Blame?

I want to learn to stay out of another person's space unless and until I've been invited into that space! Why? Because space invasion will not meet my deep-felt needs! In fact, that very intrusion carries with it the three inherent dangers we've just discussed:

1. It encourages irresponsibility.
2. It builds walls.
3. It fosters dependency.

Two additional irritants make it even more logical to avoid invading another's space. First, when I do tell people what to do, and then they don't do it, I'm frustrated. At that point I realize that I don't control what's happening anyway.

And a second thing . . . when people *do* take my advice and it turns out badly, who gets blamed? You've got it. I do!

A Happier Ending

As we bridge now from the things to *avoid* and begin looking at the things to *learn* in building a relationship, let's back up and take another look at the "cheating" episode we considered earlier.

What would have happened if the father had said to his son, "Thanks for sharing with me about this struggle you're facing. It's a tough one, and I really appreciate the trust you demonstrate by confiding in me." *Period.*

How would the son have felt? "Dad understands. It was a risk, but I did the right thing by telling him. I can tell he loves me by the way he sticks with me even when I blow it. It's great to have a dad who listens . . . and who cares."

This time the father has supported his son. He has not condoned his cheating, nor has he judged it. After all, the son knew a long time ago what his father thought about cheating. And that is what makes the father's acceptance of his child, not his child's behavior, so special at a time like this. When he needed a father to listen and understand, Dad was there.

An incident of shame in the young man's life has been allowed to forge a tighter bond between father and son.

♦ Interaction ♦

Consider the most important human relationship in your life at this time. Examine whether or not you are intruding into the other person's space. Are you allowing your own space to be invaded?

One way to conduct this examination is to list all the "shoulds" you are imposing in the relationship. Next consider the "shoulds" that are being imposed upon you.

For example, "My mate should not disagree with me when I discipline the children," or "I must call and tell my spouse if
I'm not going to be home at the anticipated
time."

How can you work with these "shoulds"?
Talk to yourself this way. "It would be nice if
. . . ," but it isn't a "has to." When you think
about it, there really are very few "has to's" in
life.

If this works well for you, try the process in
one or two other significant relationships.

The second part of this assignment is to
develop a list of ways you can learn to be
more receptive and supportive of that meaningful person in your life. Try to get at least
five suggestions written down. Select one or
preferably two to try. Write a paragraph on
the results in your journal. Include how the
experience made you feel.

- Avoid Withdrawing ▰▰▰▰▰◣
  - Avoid Placating ▰▰▰▰▰◣
    - Avoid Intruding ▰▰▰▰◣

    - ● **Learn Giving** ▰▰▰▰▰▰▱
  - Learn Receiving ══════
  - Learn Inviting ══════
- Learn Contributing ══════

Chapter 5

Learn Giving
—Find the Richer Way of Life—

IN DOUG'S MIND, reconciliation with Angela is a huge challenge. A contest. And he wants to win. He *has* to win, because if he can't win . . . well, there is no other option. Losing is unthinkable. He'd rather die.

Have you ever felt that kind of desperation? Schemes, plans, ideas . . . searching and searching for ways to "win" . . . ways to get that special someone to like you again. Ordinarily you wouldn't see yourself as a "desperate" person, and neither would anyone else. In every other area of life you may find success within easy reach, yet in this one relationship, the thing that means the most to you, you find yourself in a twenty-four-hour nightmare of blind alleys, box canyons, and dead ends.

Angela, who had gathered her resolve to leave and now feels settled about it, will read

"Friendship thrives on giving, not competition."

Doug's pleas and plots as manipulative. It will confirm her opinion of his selfishness.

Doug feels rising frustration, bordering on panic, that none of his carefully-laid plans are working. "Why won't Angela listen? Why won't she try to understand? What kind of hoops does she want me to jump through, anyway?"

And so Doug tries harder . . . and Angela retreats farther. The more he tries to persuade, cajole, threaten, or entice his estranged wife to return, the more determined she seems to have nothing to do with him.

Doug's life yo-yos from despair ("She won't let me see her") to soaring hope ("She didn't hang up on me last night"). He sees himself as either "winning" or "losing." In his eyes, it's definitely black or white, either/or, advance in victory or retreat in defeat.

And yet Doug does have another option. It is something besides competing or giving in, something beyond winning or losing. There is a third way. It is an option he may scoff at. And yet it is a powerful choice, with enough dynamic to not only affect his relationship with Angela but to transform his very life.

It is the option of giving.

The Way to Keep Filling Your Life

Learn to give, for it deepens your relationship. Friendship thrives on giving, not competition. Giving comes from my being—who I am. Competition comes from my performance—what I do.

What Doug has trouble realizing is that

friendship and affection cannot be won by negotiation or collective bargaining. He can't "make" Angela love him again.

Even in a power-oriented society such as the one in which we live, each man and woman is responsible for his or her own feelings. I don't control your feelings and you don't control mine.

From one point of view, that thought is encouraging. If someone likes me, it is because that individual has chosen to like me. In other ways, however, it is difficult to accept. We're so achievement-oriented. We've been told all our lives that the way to obtain something in this world is to work for it, to bring all our energies to bear on that object until it is ours, until we've earned it. But there is nothing I can do to earn friendship. I can't buy it. I can't outsmart, outwork, outdrive, or out-talk anyone to seize it. If it happens at all, it will be because someone has simply given it to me. And that's humbling.

Giving is not buying. Real giving has no strings attached. It has no "I gave you this so you owe me that" stuck on the end. It has no conditions to meet, no hidden agenda, no camouflaged hooks.

And the results? The outcome often defies logic. Although I give and give, and feel at times that I'll pump myself dry from all the giving, I find that my inner stores are undiminished. My life is full. I have yet more to give.

Jesus demonstrated that principle on a remote stretch of coastline among a vast throng of people (Luke 9). Thousands of

"Real giving . . . has no conditions to meet, no hidden agenda, no camouflaged hooks."

"Jesus floored them with a reply: 'You give them something to eat.' "

men, women, and children from towns and villages and farms throughout Galilee had followed the Nazarene to this lonely place and listened spellbound as He spoke. They were open, eager to learn, and Jesus poured Himself out to them, "teaching them many things."

The people couldn't seem to get enough of this refreshing, highly unusual Rabbi. And so the hours sped by and the shadows lengthened and the sun began to edge its way toward the horizon.

Finally the disciples awakened to their "civic responsibility." The Master, obviously caught up in His teaching, had apparently forgotten the practical aspects of their situation. Here they were, miles from town or village, with a huge gathering of people before them—people who would soon be missing their dinners.

Sober-faced, they approached their Leader with a little down-to-earth counsel.

"Send the people away so they can go to the surrounding countryside and villages and get something to eat," they suggested.

Without even hesitating, Jesus floored them with a reply. "You give them something to eat."

What ever could He be talking about? One of the more practical souls among their number tactfully reminded the Master that to furnish even one meal for a mob this massive would take eight months of a man's wages.

In addition, a quick inventory of available food turned up no more than five small loaves of bread and two modest fish. With these seemingly meager resources in hand, Jesus blessed the food, divided it up, and gave it to His men to distribute.

Everyone had plenty to eat that evening. And after the whole crowd had eaten all they wanted, the stunned disciples gathered twelve baskets of leftovers.

Jesus' men must have learned many lessons that afternoon. And surely one of them must have been the fact that giving does not diminish the one who gives.

". . . giving does not diminish the one who gives."

When Living Becomes Giving

I am enriched when I choose to give. The more I give the more I have to give. Giving fulfills me and expands me.

Jesus, in His earthly life, chose to neither compete nor give in. He didn't measure life in those terms at all. He just gave. Of Himself. Out of the fathomless depths of Who He was. Out of His very being.

And you and I have that option as well. Instead of struggling and competing, we can *give*. Instead of throwing up our hands and giving in, we can *give*. It doesn't necessarily mean "winning" in a relationship. Nor will the bottom line necessarily mean "losing." It can't be regarded as a strategy that will show up in the "box scores" of how many friends you've gathered and maintained. On the other hand, it can't help affecting your relationships for the simple reason that it affects you.

You become different. Your focus

"Love calls me . . . to share out of the wealth of who I am."

changes. And how many truly giving, loving, unselfish people do you know who lack for friends?

Many of us hesitate to give out of fear that someone will take advantage of us or walk all over us. Giving, in fact, runs counter to the "look out for yourself" philosophy which saturates the music and thinking of our culture. So many of our acquaintances seem to face opportunities with a "What's in it for me?" kind of attitude.

Yet for all of that, the principle stands: *Learn to give, for it deepens your relationships.* If relationships are to become more than surface, fragile things, they must grow beyond the "this for that" mentality: "I'll allow you this much love and attention for that much love and attention." Love calls me to give and to share out of the wealth of who I am, and to do so in a deliberate, intentional way.

What Is the Pay-Off?

What would this kind of giving mean for Doug and Angela? Doug may feel, "Angela doesn't deserve kindness from me. I didn't ask her to leave. I didn't want her to leave. Look at the way she has hurt me. It isn't fair. She certainly hasn't earned any gifts of love from me."

If I thought he would listen, I might relate to this distressed young client a story about another undeserving, ungrateful, totally unworthy individual. Here was a young man who demanded his share of the family inheritance from his father, traveled to a distant place, and squandered it all.

Destitute and broken, this foolish son came dragging back home. And the father? Well, think of the hell he'd been through. Think of the sorrow, the days of self-searching despair, the long evenings of aching loneliness. Surely this son of his deserved nothing but scorn and indifference. How could you give to someone who had so recklessly rejected you, who had so callously ignored your trauma of grief and loss. What did he deserve from his dad? Absolutely nothing. Zilch.

And yet the father deliberately chose a different response. Can we read the familiar words without feeling the pulse of their emotion?

"While he was still a long way off, his father saw him and was filled with compassion for him; he ran to his son, threw his arms around him and kissed him" (Luke 15:20).

There might have been bitter scoldings at home that night. Or deathly silence. Or cold rejection. Instead, there was feasting. And warmth. And dancing. And joy. And tears of gladness. And restoration. Did the young man deserve this outpouring of compassion? Not a bit of it! But his father chose to give. And everyone was the richer.

Doug faces a similar decision. He could choose to give to Angela, regardless of her decision to stay away or come home. Regardless of whether he wins or loses. He struggles with that thought, and yet . . . in the long run . . . does it really matter if Angela deserves

"There might have been bitter scoldings at home that night. . . . Instead, there was feasting."

his love? Does it? Doug could wrestle with questions such as, "What's fair?" or "Who's to blame?" for the rest of his life. But what would he have to show for it?

Only empty, bitter, *lonely* years. That's all.

Doug could also choose to quit worrying about "what is fair." He could choose to follow the ancient counsel of Paul, who wrote, "Love keeps no record of wrongs." He could quit talking about how much he loves Angela and start demonstrating that love through no-strings-attached giving.

Will it pay off? Will Angela come back if Doug gives up his expectations and invests himself in giving? Who knows? I don't. That's up to Angela.

The "payoff" may not come in the form of a mended marriage. But that's okay. Because if Doug is really giving, it is because he *wants* to, not because he *has* to. And in the meantime, he will be climbing out of destructive thought patterns of surging highs and crashing lows.

Whether Angela chooses to come back or not, Doug will be the richer when he chooses to give.

◆ Interaction ◆

Giving and loving are dynamic processes. Giving is an act of loving. Do you get tired of listening to some people say how much they love another person? I do. At times I want to respond with, "Don't tell me. Show me."

Would you like to start giving? It's a little frightening if you haven't done much of it before. It gets easier with practice. It grows like a spiral, starting with a single expression and expanding with each future gift.

Choose that special someone you want to be the recipient of your gift. Decide what it is you're going to give. It need not be tangible. An uplifting remark can be a meaningful way to give. If you are giving something tangible, you may choose to do so anonymously at first. That will help you to establish a single motive for this meaningful self-expression without any secondary motives creeping in to sap the benefits.

Observe your feelings for two or three days and then pen a brief paragraph in your personal journal about the experience.

Repeat the process as often as desired!

• Avoid Withdrawing ▰▰▰▰▰
  • Avoid Placating ▰▰▰▰▰
    • Avoid Intruding ▰▰▰▰▰▰

    • Learn Giving ▰▰▰▰▰▰
  ● **Learn Receiving** ▰▰▰▰▰▰
  • Learn Inviting ══════════
• Learn Contributing ════════

Chapter 6

Learn Receiving
—Accept What Only Others Can Give—

MISSED OPPORTUNITIES!
We've all heard, with a pang, the distressing stories . . . of searchers who called it quits within yards of a lost child . . . of prospectors who moved on when only inches from a mother lode . . . of thirst-parched adventurers who despaired and died within a stone's throw of the Amazon.

And how many "thirsty" moments and "parched" feelings have you and I endured—when we didn't have to! These were times when we simply failed to see or receive what was available, or perhaps even given, to us. So close. So within reach. And yet we missed it!

But let's accept the advice given earlier and focus on what lies ahead. We can't redo the past, so let those depressive hurts and frustrations of yesterday go. Let's build on

"Receiving can have implications beyond what you'd first imagine."

the opportunities of today . . . and of tomorrow.

And if a helpful something is within reach *today*, let's not miss it.

An important step in that process? *Learn to receive, for it deepens your relationship.*

What Happens When Others Give

"Receiving" is not "getting." You get something when you go after it. In a sense you even earn what you get. But you receive what someone else has provided for you.

It's just there. You either accept it or reject it. People feel they deserve what they "get." What people "receive," however, may or may not be deserved.

On the surface this sounds all too easy. "Receiving? I'm all for it," you laugh. "Just find me someone who wants to give!" But don't be too hasty. Receiving can have implications beyond what you'd first imagine.

Sometimes we find ourselves wrestling with self-doubt. It's difficult to receive anything at such moments. I recall the surprise of being singled out for a "special recognition award." It was at a luncheon of a professional association to which I belong. What a surprise! After the master of ceremonies gave a little speech complimenting me for some of my efforts, he called me to the platform to present me with a beautiful plaque.

The warm, genuine applause rang in my ears as I weaved through the tables of my smiling colleagues to get to the front. But you know . . . I never really received the award that day. Oh, I reached out and took it. I gave an appreciative, self-evasive little speech. I even carried the plaque to my hotel room that night and set it by my bed. But I couldn't *receive* it. My mind was too crowded with tumultuous thoughts and emotions. "Do you really deserve that award, Gordon? Did they really mean that applause . . . or were they just being polite? Would they still have given you the award if they'd known this . . . or this . . . or that?"

I missed something that night. Something that was close. Something that was available. Something that was being freely extended to me. And something that I very much wanted. It was the esteem of my friends and colleagues, and it eluded my grasp. I returned to my hotel room feeling empty and alone.

What, then, is an appropriate response when someone wants to give me something? Don't "take" it. Learn to receive it! "Taking" and "getting" are words of competition, linked to what I do. "Receiving" and "giving" are words of identity, linked to who I am.

A sincere "thank you" is all that's needed. But what is a sincere thank you? It's one that communicates "I appreciate you and this expression of thoughtfulness that comes from you to me."

This kind of receiving rules out feelings of obligation ("What should I say? What do they want?"). It rules out feelings of guilt ("I'm not worthy"). It rules out feelings of conceit ("It's the least they could do after all I've done"). It has no thought of getting even

> *"Don't 'take' it. Learn to receive it!"*

*"Learning
to receive
both the
good and
the bad,
both the joys
and the sor-
rows, will
deepen your
relation-
ships."*

or paying back. It is not taking something because I've earned it. It is opening my arms
and heart to receive something from the
arms and heart of someone who chooses to
give it to me.

There is, however, another side to this
matter of receiving. And it isn't all positive.
Imagine this delicate situation: A grim-
looking internist calls your friend into her
office and reveals a devastating discovery.
Your friend has cancer in several vital or-
gans. Surgery is impossible. It's only a matter
of time. Maybe six months . . . perhaps as
long as a year. Your friend comes to you and
shares the fear and dread of dying. How do
you respond?

This, too, is from the heart of someone
who chooses to give to you . . . only this time
it is not warm recognition or words of appreciation and affection. This time it is sorrow. Can you, in turn, open your arms and
heart to receive this news and resign yourself
to the probable events of the coming year? It
would be possible to turn away such harsh
tidings, to think "It can't really be true" or
"Things like this don't happen to people I
know" or "If I stop thinking about it, it might
go away." It would be possible to fill your
mind and hours with other things, other activities, and leave your friend to struggle
alone.

Whatever path you choose, the truth re-
mains: Learning to receive both the good
and the bad, both the joys and the sorrows,
will deepen your relationships.

It is not selfish to receive—even the good

things. Nor are you doing your friends any favor when you decline to receive what they offer. Indeed, when we make such a refusal, we are denying that person's need to give. A giver needs a receiver, just like a baseball pitcher needs a catcher.

"A failure to receive can add up to a failure to grow."

When Receiving Means Growing

A failure to receive can add up to a failure to grow. It's as though we deliberately walked by all of the flowers we've ever been close to, refusing to appreciate their beauty, refusing to enjoy their fragrance, refusing to feel the cool dew drops that cling to their petals. All of those flowers, created for our enjoyment, are lost to us! It is, of course, our choice. Yet how unspeakably sad to live in a world without flowers . . . when we don't have to.

When I chose to develop a personal relationship with Jesus Christ, I chose to receive what He had given. That's where it started.

"He came unto his own (people), and his own (people) received him not. But as many as received him, to them gave he power to become the sons of God" (John 1:11-12, KJV).

My relationship with God began by receiving. And it is deepened as I receive from Him and He receives from me.

That kind of receiving takes some thought and some readjustment of perspective. A year ago I sprained my ankle jogging on a dark, wet Oregon morning. I tripped, the ankle turned, the pain shot up my leg, and

... well, I really get twinges just thinking about it. But I can tell you this: I'm thankful the ankle is healed. I'm thankful that I don't have to hobble around and groan for the rest of my life. It's as though it had never happened. The swelling has gone. It isn't purple anymore. I can walk and even run without pain.

Now the physical renewal of my left ankle could be viewed rather matter-of-factly as the natural consequence of time and the recuperative powers of the body. I could look at it that way. But I could also see that healing is a gift to be received from a gracious, compassionate God. I choose to see it the latter way. And as I do, it deepens my appreciation for Who He is and what He has done for me. I love Him that much more. Our relationship is that much deeper.

Either view has, in one sense, the same result. Either way, my ankle is once again strong and usable. And yet when I see the healing as a loving gift that someone else has provided for me, I am able to enjoy an added relational benefit. I find closeness in my heart to God as well as healing in my body. And I become more and more aware of the great kindness of a God who loves and cares for me.

What a difference this can make to the "common" events of everyday living. I came closer to the truth of Paul's amazing counsel to the Thessalonians: "Be joyful always; pray continually; give thanks in all circumstances, for this is God's will for you in Christ Jesus" (1 Thessalonians 5:16-18).

Receiving a Person, Not His Irresponsible Behavior

Let's bring receiving back, however, to the level of friend to friend. What happens when a friend engages in activity which I cannot accept? How can I receive from that person when he or she is engaged in behavior I cannot condone? At that point we must face a crucial distinction: I may accept *who a person is* although I may not choose to accept *what that person does.*

It is not my responsibility to change what any responsible person does!

As a parent, I may work to change behavior in my children who have not yet learned to be responsible. That's part of parenting.

Other relationships, however, are considered on a different level . . . spouse to spouse . . . friend to friend—these are relationships between responsible persons. And developing better relationships with these individuals is a matter of receiving who a person is whether or not I accept or reject what that person does. It does *not* help a relationship when I try to get my friend or spouse to change what he or she does.

"But you said 'responsible' person," you might argue. "I have a relationship with someone who is irresponsible, so I can try to change what she or he is doing."

Sure. You can try. But what kind of relationship do you want? Do you want a "parenting" type of relationship where you accept the task of teaching a friend or spouse to be responsible?

"I may accept who a person is although I may not choose to accept what that person does."

Remember Sarah and Randy in chapter 4? Randy would clink glasses with his buddies at the tavern all evening, then awaken his wife to come drive him home. And all of Sarah's well-intentioned efforts to "make Randy responsible" had been backfiring.

Sarah will be happier when she faces up to the fact that it is not her responsibility to persuade Randy to stop drinking and carousing. She doesn't have to accept his drinking, and she certainly doesn't need to feel obligated to run the "rescue van" to bring him home every night.

The real question Sarah faces is this: Does she choose to *break* the relationship with Randy and move out, or to *build* that relationship, in spite of his irresponsible behavior?

If she chooses to build the relationship, she will have to find it in her heart to receive who he is—and to appreciate him. She will not close her eyes to his offensive and unacceptable behaviors. She will choose to focus on the good in her husband as she develops tolerance for the behaviors in Randy which bother her.

Who knows? Sarah's ability to receive Randy for who he is in spite of what he does could have some sobering effects.

◆ Interaction ◆

Ask yourself the question, "In what ways have I failed to receive the benefits obtainable in my relationship(s)?" Have a specific "someone" in mind as you think this over.

Two possibilities that you won't want to overlook are (1) "To what extent have I failed to receive from the other person because I have put myself down?" and (2) "Have I been upset with certain behaviors in the other person and thus neglected to see the positive things that individual provides for me?"

Are you a "walking apology"? You need not be! In your journal, describe three situations where you have cheated yourself by failing to acknowledge your strengths. Next determine at least two alternative responses to each of these situations. Write the responses down so you have a record to which you can be accountable.

Think of that special someone in your life that you want to build a deeper relationship with. Perhaps you've been critical of that person in one or more ways. Instead of focusing on those things that bother you, make a list of the ten things you admire most in that individual. Let your mind dwell on these attributes and learn to appreciate each of them.

- Avoid Withdrawing ▰▰▰▰▰▰
  - Avoid Placating ▰▰▰▰▰▰
    - Avoid Intruding ▰▰▰▰▰▰

  - Learn Giving ▰▰▰▰▰▰▰
  - Learn Receiving ▰▰▰▰▰▰
  - ● **Learn Inviting** ▰▰▰▰▰▰▰
- Learn Contributing ════════

Chapter 7

Learn Inviting
—Ask Others in to Get Acquainted—

BERT HAS HIS EYE on Jacqueline.

"She," says Bert, "is the one for me. Oh my, the way the sunlight touches her hair . . . that smile . . . I adore her."

It's spring, of course, and Bert's emotions are running high. He could almost write poetry. He could almost compose a ballad. He could almost, well, send some roses from the local florist.

And so the doorbell rings at Jacqueline's house and the florist hands her a half dozen long-stemmed beauties in a pink-ribboned box. Now that surprise is enough to send Jacqueline's emotions soaring. How romantic! And how *mysterious*. Bert has neglected to enclose a card.

Very much moved by the anonymous gift, Jacqueline brings down that "special" vase from the top shelf of the cupboard. She

"Learn to invite, for it deepens your relationships."

carefully trims the roses, arranges them, and places them at the center of a sunsplashed table in her dining room. They're so pretty, but . . . it's almost sad . . . there is no one to thank.

Bert has given, Jacqueline has received, yet . . . the relationship hasn't deepened at all. An appreciative lady named Jacqueline has no opportunity to get acquainted with a generous man named Bert.

"Do I Know You?"

Do you ever get that kind of feeling even with someone you "know"? It comes with a touch of sadness. You're certainly acquainted with the individual. You know a lot about him or her. But do you *know* that person? It's debatable.

I've spoken with husbands and wives who've spent years living together. And yet each would affirm, "I'm not sure I really know my mate."

You've probably even heard it said, "That person is hard to get to know." It's not meant to be a negative or critical comment. And it isn't said in anger. It's just a statement about a feeling.

Has anyone ever said that to you? "I don't know you very well. When I'm with you, I don't know what you're thinking or feeling. I have no idea what's going on inside your head . . . or heart."

These wistful reflections bring us to a vital principle: *Learn to invite, for it deepens your relationship.*

To invite another is to share with that person. You are bringing him or her into your own space and asking that person to look around. The walls of concealment begin to fade as you invite your friend or spouse to browse the library of your dreams, hopes, goals, and uncertainties.

Inviting starts with the important principle that began this book: accepting who I am and liking that person.

I will be very reluctant to let other people see who I am when I refuse to accept myself. Once that step of self-acceptance has been taken, however, this very crucial relation-building step is open to me. I can go beyond talking about what I do and begin to reveal who I really am.

"The walls . . . begin to fade as you invite your friend or spouse to browse the library of your dreams."

"Come, and You Will See . . ."

The earthly ministry of Jesus contained many invitations in its short span of three years. Consider one of His first:

> The next day John was there again with two of his disciples. When he saw Jesus passing by, he said, "Look, the Lamb of God!"
>
> When the two disciples heard him say this, they followed Jesus. Turning around, Jesus saw them following and asked, "What do you want?"
>
> They said, "Rabbi" (which means Teacher), "where are you staying?"
>
> "Come," he replied, "and you will see."

"The Savior opened His thoughts and feelings to let men and women in."

So they went and saw where he was staying, and spent that day with him (John 1:35-39).

One of those former disciples of the Baptist's was Andrew, who responded to the invitation by committing his life to following the Galilean. Andrew in turn invited his brother Peter to meet Jesus. And so it went. Christ's simple "Come" sparked a chain reaction of events which launched Him into the public ministry.

I find myself responding again and again to another of the Lord's invitations in the book of Matthew. Jesus had been speaking of the dark days which lay ahead for the cities which had rejected His ministry. And in His heart, Jesus knew that there would be dark days ahead for the ones who had followed Him as well. Looking into the faces of those He loved so dearly, He extended this gracious invitation:

> "Come to me, all you who are weary and burdened, and I will give you rest. Take my yoke upon you and learn from me, for I am gentle and humble in heart, and you will find rest for your souls. For my yoke is easy and my burden is light" (Matthew 11:28-30).

What a beautiful transparency. The Savior opened His thoughts and feelings to let men and women in. And because we hold His Word in our hands, He says the same to us. "Look Me over. What do you think? Am I for real? If so, I invite you to build a better relationship with Me. Follow Me . . . become My disciples and My friend."

But What if Someone Says "No"?

There were times when people chose not to respond to Christ's invitation. Some of these incidents, too, are recorded in Scripture. Mark 10:17-22 relates the story of a very wealthy young man who seemed to be interested in what the Galilean had to offer. They talked. The gospel writer relates that Jesus felt love for this evidently sincere youth. The Lord's invitation, however, sent a surge of ice water through the young ruler's veins.

"Jesus did not run after him down the dusty lane."

"Go," said Jesus, "sell everything you have and give to the poor, and you will have treasure in heaven. Then come, follow me" (Mark 10:21).

The Bible tells us that the young man's face fell. Turning his back on the Lord of life, he went back to his cold stacks of gold, his "great wealth."

Jesus did not run after him down the dusty lane. He did not shout, "Wait! You apparently don't understand. Please . . . reconsider!"

No, Jesus let him go. He imposed no demands. It was just an invitation. The man went on his way and Jesus continued His teaching.

Invitations seem to come so easily for children. They don't spend time fretting about possible negative responses. Untroubled by the relational subtleties and complexities that worry their elders, kids simply blurt out their desires.

"Invitations are not schemes to persuade another person to like me."

Observe the unabashed joy and enthusiasm of the child who shouts across the yard to her friend:

"Can you come over to my house and play?"

And then there are those confrontive questions that get right down to the issue:

"Do you want to be my friend? I want to be your friend. Do you want to be mine?"

Learn to invite, for it deepens your relationship.

What happens when you or I extend an invitation and get turned down? It's not too bad when it happens now and then, but how much rejection can one person stand?

"How long," you may be asking, "can I keep giving and inviting when there's no reciprocation? It's like trying to dance with a brick wall."

Our response to a declined invitation may reveal much about the true nature of that invitation. If you find yourself getting angry or upset because someone refuses to accept your invitation, then perhaps it wasn't a genuine invitation at all. Perhaps it was a demand, just masquerading as an invitation.

Invitations are not "schemes" to persuade another person to like me. When I invite another into my space and open the door to my thinking and feeling, it is without thought of "bait." Bait, after all, is something you use in a trap. It implies "I gotcha" once I lure you in. No, true invitations reject the spider-and-fly mentality. True invitations do not limit the invited one's freedom of choice.

When you choose to decline my invitation, I don't need to feel down. You didn't reject *me,* just my invitation. If, however, you choose to receive my invitation and walk through the open door into my space, our relationship will be deepened. You will know me better.

Safe . . . and Lonely

Building better relationships requires effort . . . and risk.

We can all look back on times when we opened that inner door of our thoughts and feelings to someone and now wish we had not. They didn't wipe their feet when they came in. They weren't careful with the furniture. They broke some of the fragile things we had cherished. They laughed at some of the furnishings we had thought beautiful. And then they left. And we slammed the door behind them.

Encounters like those leave scars, don't they? We're careful about opening that door again, to anyone. We want to peek through the little hole and decide if that person is "okay" first. We're not so sure that we want to unlatch all those deadbolts and chains.

As you read these words you might be thinking about a locked and bolted door in your own life. Perhaps you felt you had to take precautions after one or more painful incidents in your past.

Doors, however, can be unlocked and opened. Even doors with deadbolts and chains and bars. Even doors that were painted shut years ago.

It's risky. But the fresh air is delightful.

"Doors can be unlocked and opened. Even doors with deadbolts and chains and bars."

The sunlight can transform a whole room. Why not plan a careful, deliberate "open house" for a special someone . . . soon. Invite another person to step over the threshold for a moment or two.

As you choose to invite, you build better relationships. There's something beautiful about an open door.

◆ Interaction ◆

It hurts to get "burned" in a relationship. As you have read in these pages, some of you recognize the "shell" you have built around yourself.

Perhaps you were sexually molested by a father or uncle. There may have been other deep hurts that are difficult to even think about. What could you do when you were enduring those painful moments? You withdrew, gave in, traveled in your mind to another place when your feet were helpless to escape the situation.

Today those hurts are walled behind the heavy door within you. No one, you vow, will ever hurt you like that again. So you keep the doors and windows locked, extend no invitations, and play it safe.

Safe. Secure. Insulated. Protected. And . . . very lonely.

Let me challenge you to build a door and to invite another person into your "shell." Plan it carefully and deliberately. Have several alternatives in mind as you contemplate your plan. Don't reveal any more than you choose at one time. As you gain confidence in your okayness, you will be able to risk a little more.

Keep a record in your journal of the progress you are making. When you feel discouraged, go back and examine to see what alternatives can improve the plan. Inviting and giving will go together well, but it won't happen until you build a door.

That is your choice!

"There's something beautiful about an open door."

• Avoid Withdrawing ▰▰▰▰▰▰
  • Avoid Placating ▰▰▰▰▰▰
    • Avoid Intruding ▰▰▰▰▰

      • Learn Giving ▰▰▰▰▰▰▶
      • Learn Receiving ▰▰▰▰▰▶
    • Learn Inviting ▰▰▰▰▰▰▶
  • Learn Contributing ▰▰▰▰▰▶

Chapter 8

Learn Contributing
—Reduce the Distance through Shared Goals—

AFTER THE HORROR and trauma of the crucifixion, Peter decided to go back to what he knew best.

Fishing.

He invited four other disciples of the slain Nazarene to join him.

They spent a long, weary night on the Sea of Tiberias. Talk about gloomy hours on a dark lake. The focus of their lives for three amazing years had been swept away by a screaming mob. "Crucify Him!" still echoed in their pain-filled memories . . . if they chose to remember at all.

He was gone. That's all that mattered. Plans, hopes, and longings died with Him. All of them were gone. All had died.

Still . . . there was fishing.

But apparently there were *no fish!* After a whole night at the nets and oars, they had not even come up with one fish for breakfast.

Someone stood on the shore watching them. He was hardly more than a silhouette in the pre-dawn twilight.

"Friends," called the stranger, "haven't you any fish?"

"No."

(Who was that beachwalker anyway? And what did he care?)

"Throw your net on the right side of the boat," he shouted, "and you will find some."

As the disciples followed the man's suggestion, it seemed as though every fish in the lake had found its way into their nets. The nets were so full it took all their strength just to tow them ashore.

The final chapter of the book of John reveals that the concerned stranger was none other than their resurrected Lord.

But why did Jesus do that? Why did He help them to achieve their goal of catching fish? It would have seemed more logical if He had simply stridden across the water, climbed into the boat, and chided them for their doubt. How could they so quickly "abandon the cause" and return to their old occupation?

Christ, however, did not scold them. By choosing that particular means to identify Himself, He supported their efforts. He helped them to accomplish something they had decided, for that particular night, was important.

"We Shall Overcome" . . . Together

This, of course, was only one of many occasions when Christ chose to contribute to the lives of His followers. He had done it many times before in many ways.

He still does. And so can we.

Learn to contribute, for it deepens your relationships.

When I contribute to someone from my own resources, I support and help that individual to reach one of his or her goals. We become a team. And as I help my friend accomplish something he or she feels to be important, we draw closer together.

This must describe some of the emotion experienced by the civil rights marchers of the early 1960s. In those days it was more than a gathering of a dozen or more special interest groups espousing a multitude of disparate causes under the general banner of "rights." It was quite the opposite. Distinctions melted. People came together. Whites and blacks, young and old, men and women, Northerners and Southerners.

And it wasn't "causes" that brought them together, it was the *cause.* Not movements, but the *movement.* Facing danger and violence and hatred and scorn, they linked arms as well as hearts to share in the vision of a man who said, "I have a dream. . . ." They, too, had that dream. And because they shared that singular objective, they loved that man—and each other—all the more. They would pay the price, invest the time,

"People who share goals draw together."

travel the miles, face the hatred, and always cling to the dream. The cause would not die. Together they would overcome.

People who share goals draw together. It could be members of a high school football team, workers in a political campaign, or a husband and wife who save together for a week in the sun. Shared goals create a magnetism.

Do you want to get close to another person? Be patient. Wait until you have been invited into that person's thoughts and feelings. Once that invitation has been extended and you find yourself over the threshold and through the door, take a careful look around. What has that individual set his or her heart on? Now . . . what can you *contribute* to help that friend achieve the goal? As you contribute, you will find that you have drawn closer to your friend. You have deepened the relationship.

"Help Me to Be What I Want to Be!"

Bill is a sophomore in high school. Dad is frustrated because Bill has flunked English and biology. And for that matter, he's not doing real hot in algebra. Mom has talked to the teachers, the counselor, other parents, and anyone who would listen in her search for clues to better the situation. The parents have exhausted every approach they can think of: bribes, groundings, humiliations, threats, emotional appeals . . . and all with the same effort. Precisely zero.

Bill, however, shrugs it all off. His expression and tone of voice reflect a profound absence of concern. He just doesn't care and nothing seems to move him. So what do you do with a kid like that?

Listen to the parents. To hear them talk you would think they were applying all that pressure for Bill's sake. You will hear them mention the sacrifices they have made on his behalf and the incredible efforts they have extended to help him achieve "important goals."

Whose goals? Why, *their* goals. For him. What they want him to be and do.

Does that give you a clue as to where the problem lies?

These parents were contributing to Bill, and they were considering worthy goals . . . but they were not *Bill's* goals. And at that tender moment of his life, he was trying to establish a goal or two of his own. His parents, however, kept intruding into his space with their own set of objectives. Their motives were nothing but the best, but they were losing their son.

If Bill does have a goal in life right now it's this: He wants to be a better basketball player. Not much of a goal, you say. But it is Bill's goal, and it means a lot to him. He made the junior varsity squad this year as a sophomore, and he's doing pretty well.

Watch the coach as he works with Bill. It's thirty seconds before the half, and Bill makes a fundamental error in the worst place on the court . . . right in front of the bench.

The coach is beside himself. He throws down a folded towel in disgust and stomps

"Their motives were nothing but the best, but they were losing their son."

*"They've
shared a
dream . . .
and they're
closer be-
cause of it."*

halfway to the scorer's table. "Good night," he mutters, "how many times have we gone over that in practice? When's that kid gonna learn?"

The coach signals for a "time out" and the squad heads for the bench. The coach's words are to the point, and not all of them are printable. What's more, they all seem directed at just one player—Bill. Coach wants to blow up—that's obvious. He's red in the face, breathless, and grits his teeth. With exaggerated patience, however, he takes Bill through the basic play one more time while the other players look on. The buzzer sounds, signaling the end of the time out. With one last "Now you can *do* it!" the coach slaps Bill on the rump and sends him back into the game.

How does Bill respond to getting dressed down by the coach in front of his teammates and the student body? Just ask him. His response may surprise you.

"Coach? Yeah, he was really mad, wasn't he? I love him. I'd do anything he asked me to do."

Can you figure that? What makes the difference? The coach is helping Bill to achieve *Bill's* goal of becoming a good basketball player. They've shared a dream, these two. And they're closer because of it. *Learn to contribute, for it deepens your relationship.*

Reducing the Distance and Drawing Close

As you invite people into your space, you begin to reveal your hopes, your desires, your goals. One or more of your friends who have accepted your invitation may choose to contribute. They may begin to help you achieve some of those goals by joining in a team effort with you. You never asked or insisted that they help. They just chose to. And how do they feel about you? They have drawn closer to you.

So turn it around. You want to draw closer to someone. What can you do? You can begin to really listen to your friend's words. And even between the words. And if you listen long enough and carefully enough, you may begin to hear some priorities and some deeply desired goals. You may then choose to adopt one of those goals, form a team with your friend, and share in the joys as that dream comes true.

You work together, looking outward in the same direction. And the distance between you diminishes. Uniting your efforts, you find that you have also united your hearts.

"Uniting your efforts, you find that you have also united your hearts."

◆ Interaction ◆

Talk to that meaningful partner in your life. Listen carefully as you seek to find what goals that person has established for himself or herself. Select one of those goals. How can you contribute to that goal? Form a team. Let your teammate know that his or her goal is important to you and that you want to help in achieving the goal.

Keep a written record in your journal of progress. With each entry, add one or two sentences to describe your feelings toward your teammate. Upon completion of the activity, go back and read your journal entries. Did the relationship grow deeper during this time?

Chapter 9

Working for a Living . . . or for a Life?

IT WAS A LADY—I don't remember her name—who first made me ask myself this haunting question: Am I working for a *living* or for a *life?*

The lady has faded from memory. I can't even visualize her face. But the question has followed me for years. I work hard at making a living: try to do outside reading, attend seminars, plan for improvement and advancement in my field—all those things and more. Life, however, is made up of relationships . . . people . . . and how much time and effort and thought go into these? Sure, I'm a hard worker. But what really counts? Am I just working for a living . . . or am I pouring myself into a life?

The principles we've considered together (if it's in our heart to work on them) will help point us in the right direction. But how can

"How can we monitor our progress in these things?" we monitor our progress in these things? How can we tell if we're making strides or just working up a sweat on a treadmill? This final chapter will highlight two critical processes that will help us gain perspective: *evaluating* and *strategizing*.

Evaluation comes first, and deserves a few moments of your careful consideration.

Taking Stock

Imagine with me that you're ready to launch into the restaurant business. On paper, everything looks good:

- The purchase price for this restaurant is reasonable.
- The location? It's a winner. Good area and lots of traffic.
- The facilities are "Grade A"; nice eating area and dandy parking lot.
- There's already a steady clientele.
- All the suppliers are on schedule.
- The manager appears to have a good relationship with the cooks, waiters, and waitresses.
- The bank agrees to loan you the amount needed at a tolerable interest rate.

As far as you can tell, all systems appear "go," with nothing but a string of green lights and open doors. So you swallow hard, make the decision, and purchase the business.

Your decision was anything but impulsive. You took time to evaluate: to weigh the factors and to consider the options.

But things change, don't they? Move ahead five years in your imagination. A new freeway now slices its way through town a number of miles from your location. The endless flow of traffic that used to go by your restaurant has been reduced to a trickle.

Ah, but that's not all. Last winter's freak windstorm ripped up your sign, bashed in some windows, and bit big hunks out of your roof. Insurance? Well, you had underestimated how much you would need. By a bundle. Add those items to the plumbing problems in the women's room and the grill that no longer grills, and you've got some major headaches.

What about the income and expenditures for the past six months? A look at the ledger indicates the "out-go" has exceeded the income at an average rate of $500.00 per month. Your evaluation, then, indicates that something needs to be done (in a hurry!) to reduce the trend and generate a positive cash flow.

"Can I determine when a relationship is healthy . . . or beginning to fail?"

Evaluating a Relationship

When you're evaluating a business, you can employ certain standards of criteria to determine the over-all fiscal health of the enterprise. But that's a business. Can the same thing be done in a relationship? Can I determine when a relationship is healthy . . . or beginning to fail? If I can, what measurements do I use?

Measurement #1: Do each of the people in the relationship evidence good self-esteem and look for

"Healthy relation-ships do not encourage clinging de-pendency."

opportunities to find personal fulfillment?

To some extent, the health of the relationship can be determined by the health of the individuals within it. Does each person accept who he or she is and like himself? Does each person have an identity of his or her own? Would life go on for the individual if the relationship were to dissolve? Healthy relationships do not encourage clinging dependency.

Measurement #2: Have the people in the relationship developed the ability to grow in tolerance toward one another?

As I learn to accept myself for who I am, my capacity for interpersonal acceptance becomes greater. I learn to accept you and to appreciate you for who you are, independent of what you do. Be patient in this process, Carl Rogers wisely stated; "Life is a direction, not a destination." You and I will never "arrive" . . . but it is possible to grow in tolerance.

Measurement #3: Are the people in the relationship each making an effort to expand and deepen the levels of communication?

When one is running away or trying to break the relationship while the other is marching forward or trying to build the relationship, the chances are that the "expenditures" will exceed the "income." And that means bankruptcy. A relationship thrives on *mutual* effort, but moves toward extinction when one person quits.

As you evaluate the health of a relationship through these three measurements, you will be able to determine when things are progressing well, and when something needs to be done. After checking these measurements, you can choose to do your part to reverse negative trends and generate some positive communication.

Now, let's move from evaluating to *strategy*.

Charting a New Course

Go back to the restaurant and all those nagging problems. Can your business survive?

Well . . . there's some hope. Your careful analysis of the difficulties provides you with a platform to map some new strategy. You are ready to wrestle with it, starting with next year's budget. Expenditures are listed under three separate headings: (1) immediate and on-going; (2) essential for maintenance; and (3) desirable as funds are available.

You work hard over those figures, trimming back excesses so that the probability of profit can be increased. In addition to the careful planning and cutbacks, you begin to explore creative options for generating income. What are some creative options? Well, instead of cursing that new freeway, you could put up a billboard advertising your eatery. And then there's the newspaper. You could slip in some well-placed ads that grab attention with "breakfast specials" and "senior citizen discounts."

Now you're rolling! Some parts of your strategy may actually take hold, helping you

"A relationship thrives on mutual effort, but moves toward extinction when one person quits."

to reduce the deficit. Other points in the plan may backfire. But you keep at it, monitoring the situation, modifying your strategy when needed so as to gain the desired income.

If it works, your business is a success. If it fails, you go broke—or sell out before you do.

Now that's business. But we're interested in relationships! Does the "strategy" technique apply?

Applying Strategy to a Relationship

Again and again I've heard these words in the counseling office: "I'm not happy in this relationship, and I don't know if I want to continue in it."

As the discussion goes on, it is evident that the individual has not taken the time to evaluate the source of dissatisfaction. Like the restaurant owner, this unhappy partner can spot the deterioration, the damages, and the obvious weak spots. That's easy enough. But has the person been willing to ask why? Is the individual willing to look for a strategy to improve the relationship? Can he or she implement a strategy with potential to reverse the trend and bring new vitality to the relationship?

We've explored guidelines for developing such a strategy in the pages of this book. There are three things to "avoid" and four things to "learn." But be careful. A guideline is just a guideline; a guideline is not a strategy.

Let me illustrate. A guideline in business

may be: "To improve cash flow, either increase income, cut back on expenditures, or both." That is a guideline; it is not a strategy. A strategy involves a personal application of the guideline. The strategy provides the "how to" of increasing income or cutting expenditures.

Guidelines are usually general. Strategies need to be individual and specific. Different strategies, as a matter of fact, can grow out of the same guideline.

What works for someone else may not work for you. What seems so effective in one relationship may simply not apply in another.

"What seems so effective in one relationship may simply not apply in another."

The bottom line? Using the guidelines we've discussed in this book, create your own strategy to build a better relationship. If it works, you will be enriched. If it fails, you can hang on and endure the pains of emotional bankruptcy . . . or let go and move on to the next relationship.

Two Thoughts about Bridges

This book began with two brief, potent thoughts: (1) look ahead, and (2) focus on yourself.

Let's end it, then, with two ideas that relate to those thoughts.

First, *Don't cross bridges before you come to them.* Look ahead, yes. Visualize where you'd like to go and the way you'd like things to be. But remember, relationships are delicate things. They don't fare well when they're being rushed . . . or pushed . . . or forced.

"Keep the roads open."

Sure, think about tomorrow's possibilities; that's healthy. But remember that life is lived *today*. Time moves at its own pace. When the moment comes to apply your strategy, apply it. But don't rush.

Second, *don't blow up bridges*. You may find yourself tempted, at times, to focus on what someone else has "done" to you. Smarting from new wounds and aching from old ones, you may be at the point of delivering an ultimatum. "I'll give you this much time to change your behavior, and if you don't, KABOOM." There goes the bridge of relationship. Trouble is, bridges are difficult to build. Once destroyed it will be difficult, if not impossible, to build that span back again. And someday . . . some distant or not so distant day ahead . . . you may want that bridge very much. So keep the roads open.

Are you making a living . . . or a life? Build a healthy business and you can look forward to a cushy bank account, a positive balance sheet, and regular dividends. And that's good. Build better relationships and you can fill the hours, days, and years of your life with laughter and warmth and love. And that's the best of all.